Planets

Emily Kington

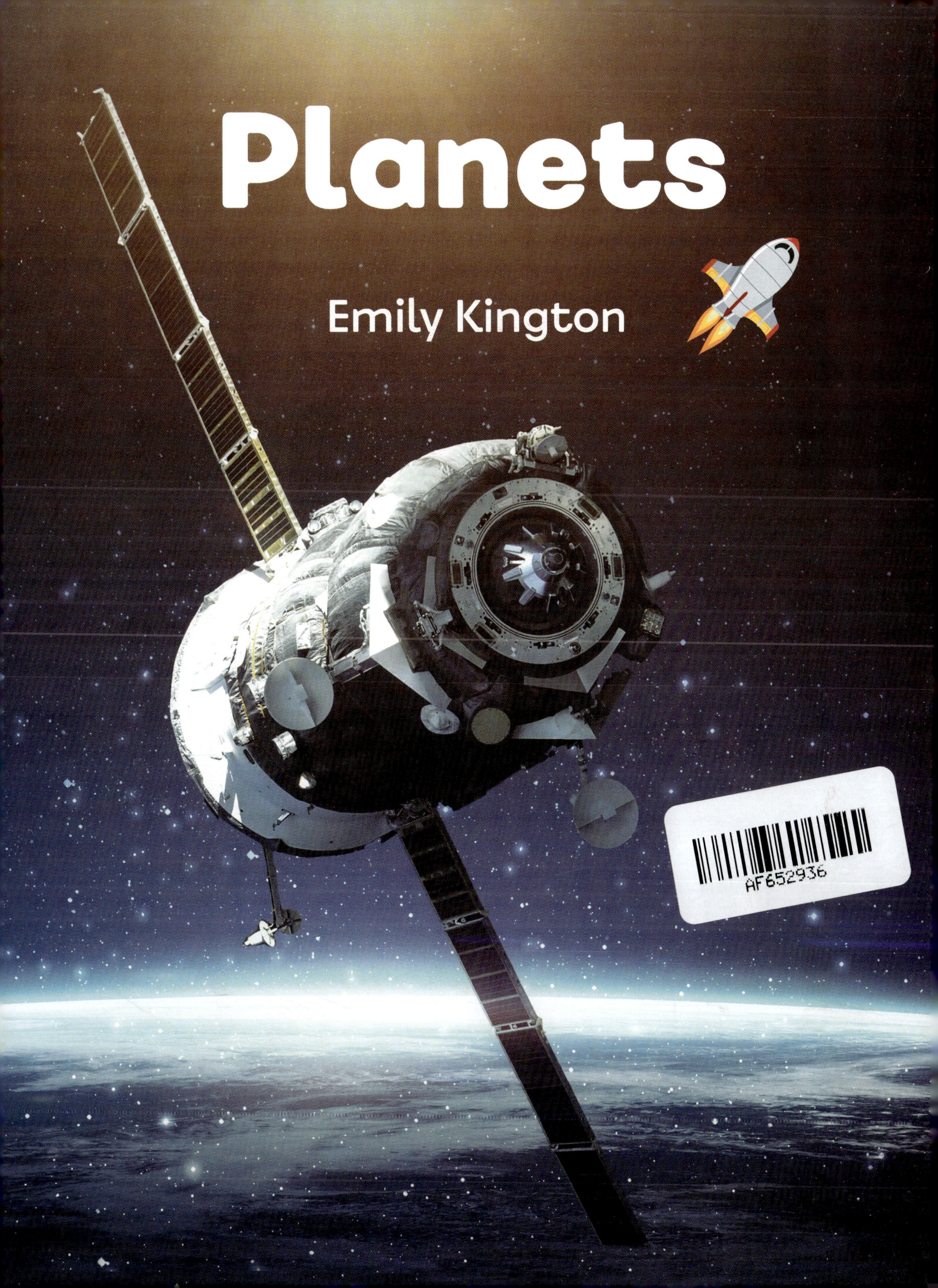

Contents

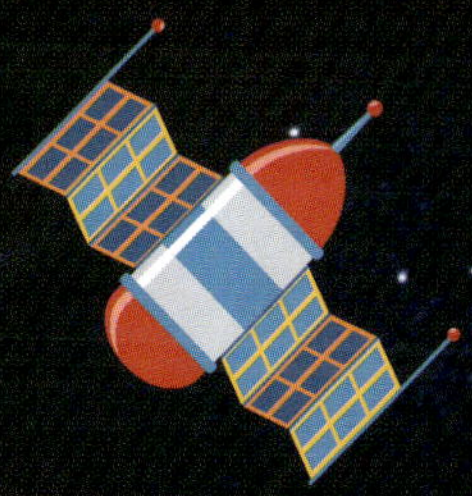

Words that appear in **bold** are explained in the glossary.

Discover more at **www.hungrytomato.com**

The Solar System

The solar system contains all of the planets, dwarf planets, moons, and other objects that travel around the Sun.

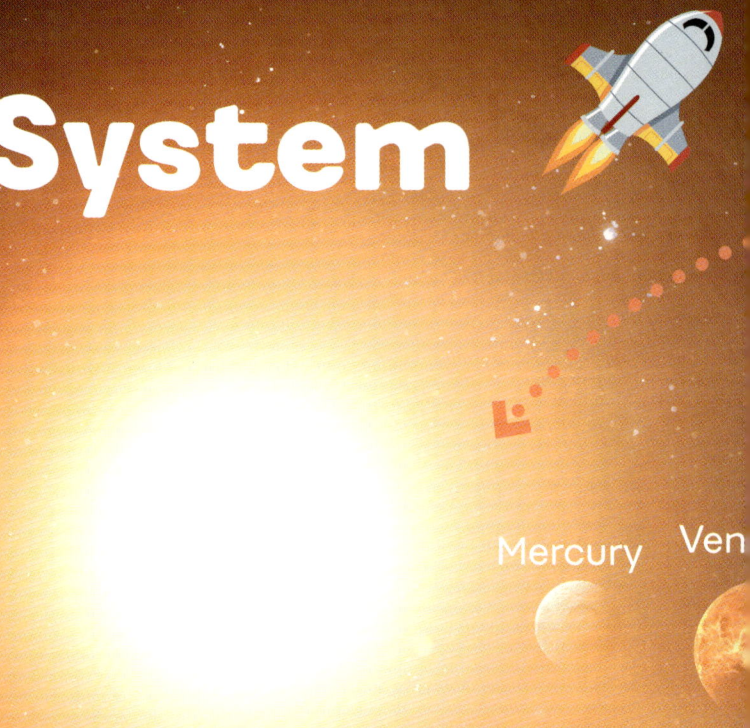

A planet's journey around the Sun is called an **orbit**. Planets stay in orbit because of a pulling force from the Sun, called **gravity**.

The Sun is a star, and without it, our solar system would not exist.

The planets all spin **(rotate)** as they orbit the Sun, one complete spin is called a **solar day.**

Mercury

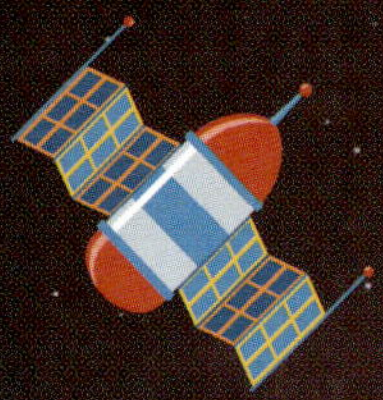

Mercury is often considered to be Earth's closest neighbour. Even though Venus gets closer, it only sweeps by us. Mercury remains nearer for longer.

A solar day on Mercury, the smallest planet, is 1,408 hours long!

Mercury is the fastest planet to orbit the Sun. Taking about 88 Earth days, it speeds around at 107,000 miles per hour!

Mercury is also the closest planet to the Sun.

Daytime temperatures on Mercury can reach 430 Celsius. It's unlikely that we would ever be able to live there!

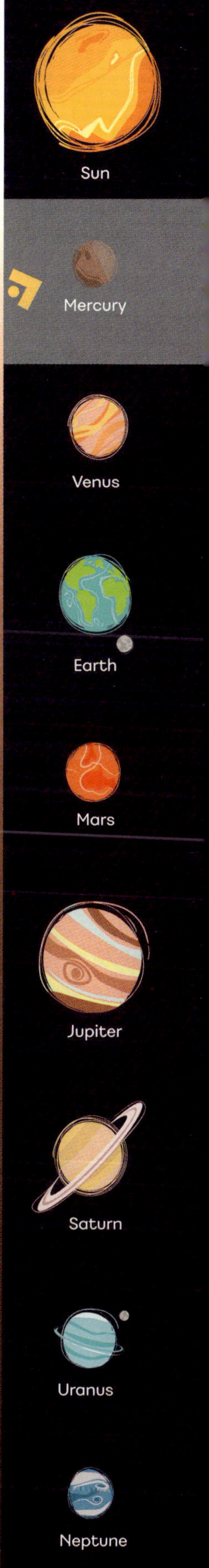

Venus

Venus is hotter than Mercury, even though it is further away from the Sun. It takes just over 224 days to orbit the Sun.

It is so hot on Venus that it would turn metals like lead into liquid!

Venus rotates in the opposite direction to the other planets.

You can sometimes see Venus at dawn. It is the brightest planet because it **reflects** the most light from the Sun.

A solar day on Venus is an incredible 5,832 hours long!

Earth

Earth is the only planet that contains liquid water. Since all living things need water to survive, it is believed to be the only planet in the solar system able to support life.

Tons of **meteoroids** crash down into **Earth's atmosphere** each year. Scientists have even found rocks from Mars.

Earth has a **magnetic field,** which helps to stop harmful particles entering our atmosphere.

A day on Earth is 24 hours long. It may not be the fastest solar day, but it's definitely not the slowest!

The Earth is sometimes called the *Blue Planet* because nearly 3/4 of Earth's surface is covered with water.

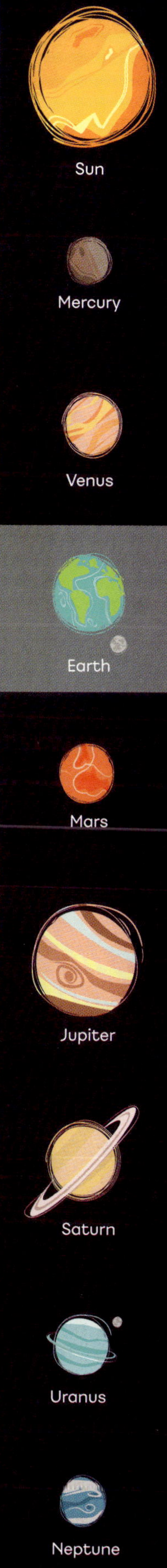

there is on Earth. If you were to jump on Mars, you would jump nearly 3 times higher!

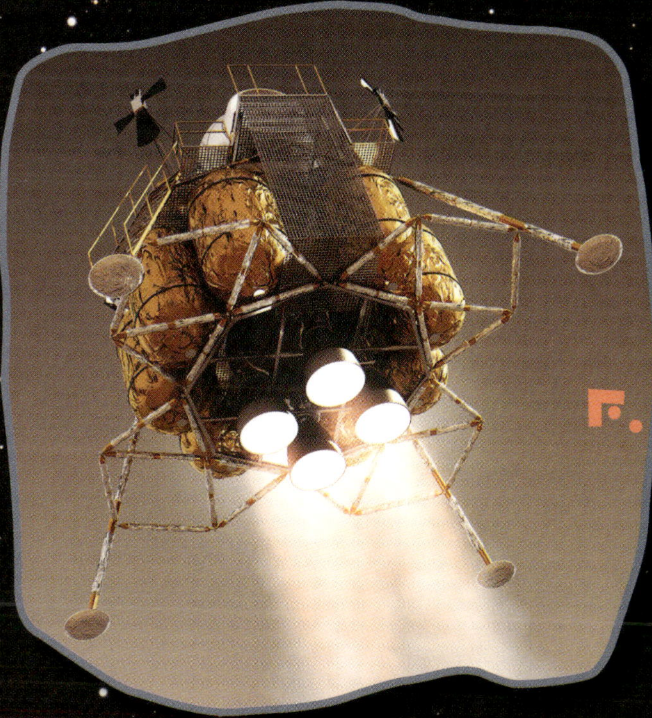

There have been many failed missions to Mars. It is the most difficult place for a lander to touch down on with a heavy load!

No humans have travelled to Mars yet, but scientists have sent robotic machines to collect data. These are called *Rovers*.

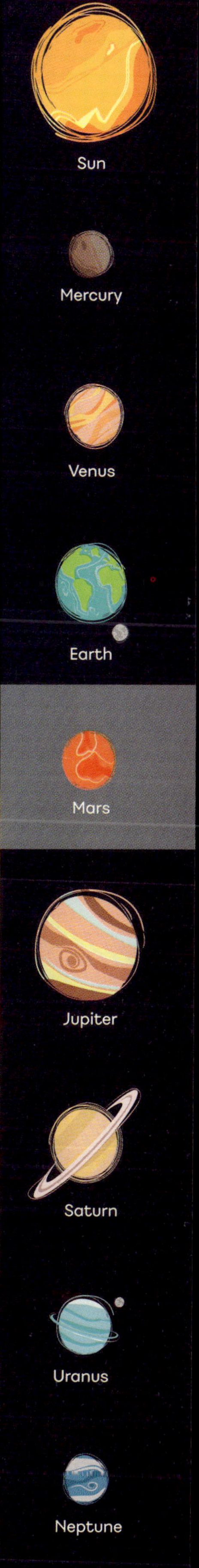

Jupiter

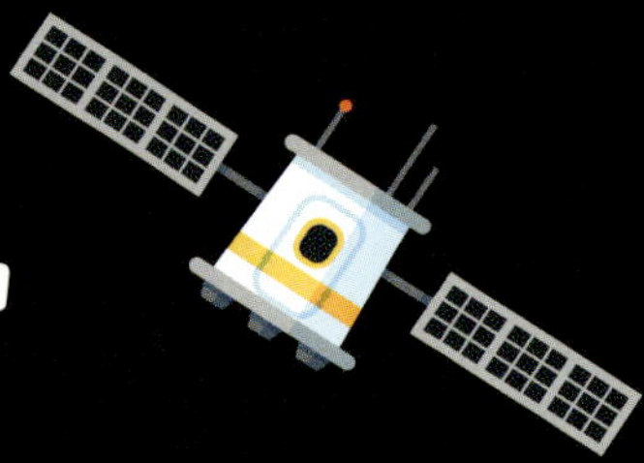

Jupiter is massive! It is twice as big as all of the other planets in the solar system put together.

There are over 60 moons that orbit Jupiter. It is also the fourth brightest natural object in the solar system.

The famous *Great Red Spot* is a giant storm, bigger than Earth, that has been raging for hundreds of years.

Jupiter is mostly made up of **gas**, which is swirled around by the great winds that circle the planet.

This giant planet has the shortest solar day, at just 10 hours long.

Saturn

Saturn is the 5th brightest object in our solar system, you will need a small telescope to see it from Earth.

Saturn is famous for its amazing rings, which are made of ice and dust that orbit the planet.

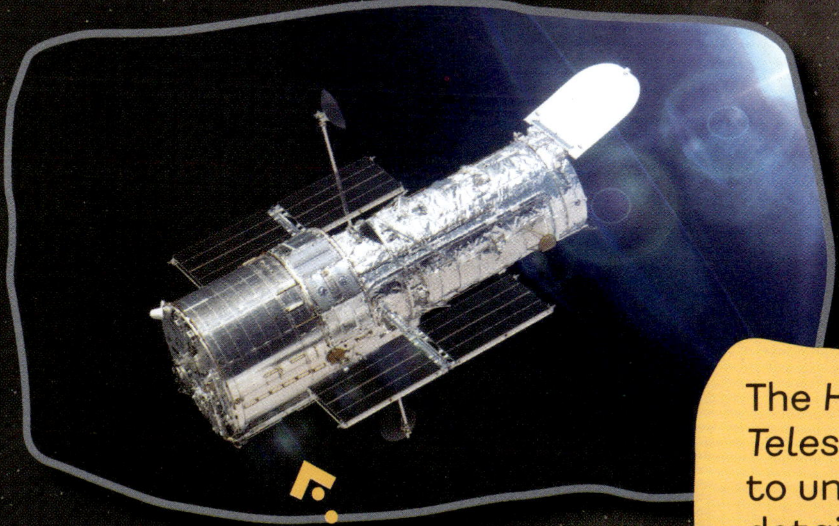

The *Hubble Space Telescope* continues to uncover new details about Saturn and its weather.

It's the 2nd largest planet in our solar system and, like Jupiter, is mostly made of gas.

A solar day on Saturn lasts for 11 hours.

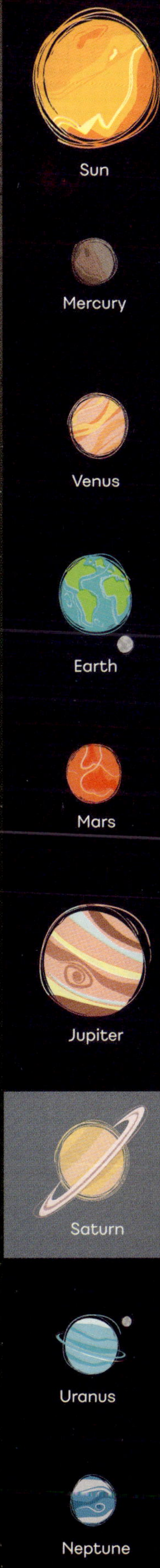

Uranus

Uranus is known as an *Ice Giant*. It was the first planet to be found with the help of a telescope, way back in 1781.

Uranus has 27 moons - here is a closer look at one of its moons.

A solar day here is just 17 hours long.

This planet is a big ball of different gases. It is likely that it would smell like rotten eggs there!

It is known as the *Sideways Planet* because it rotates on its side!

Neptune

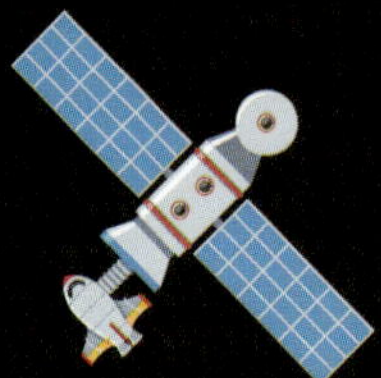

Not only is Neptune the last planet in the solar system, it's also the windiest. It was first discovered in 1846.

Voyager 2 is the only spacecraft to have passed by this distant planet.

A solar day on this lonely planet is 16 hours long.

Neptune is 30 times further away from the Sun than Earth. It is very dark and cold there!

Neptune has 6 rings but they are very faint and hard to see.

Sun

Mercury

Venus

Earth

Mars

Jupiter

Saturn

Uranus

Neptune

Pluto & the Dwarf Planets

Pluto used to be known as the 9th and smallest planet in the solar system, but astronomers have now classed it as a *Dwarf Planet*.

Pluto lies in the *Kuiper Belt* at the edge of our solar system with lots of icy, rocky objects.

Pluto takes so long to orbit the Sun that you'd have to live there for 248 Earth years before you got all the way around!

A solar day on Pluto is 153 hours long.

So far, 4 other dwarf planets have been discovered, but there could be many more.

In January 2006 Nasa launched a robot spacecraft, *New Horizons*, to study the Kuiper Belt. It finally arrived at Pluto in July 2015 ... That's a very long journey!

Glossary

Earth's atmosphere – layers of gases around the Earth, held in place by gravity (see below).

gas – a substance that is neither solid or liquid and has no fixed shape. Many gases are invisible.

gravity – a pulling force that works across space. It's the same force that causes an object to fall when you drop it.

magnetic field – an invisible space around a magnetic object, where there is a magnetic force.

meteoroid – a small natural object, such as a rock or metal, that travels through outer space.

orbit – the path taken by one object circling around another object in space.

reflects – When light bounces off the surface of an object, it is reflected.

rotation (rotate) – when something spins around a point located at its centre. Earth makes one full rotation every day.

solar day - the time it takes for a planet to make one full rotation (see above), shifting from day to night as it moves in and out of the sun's rays.

Picture Credits
(abbreviations: t = top; b = bottom; m = middle; l = left; r = right; bg = background)

3Dsculptor 13tl; AleksandrMorrisovich 18m; bluecrayola 8bg; d3verro 1tr, 3tm, 4tr, 6tm, 12tm, 16tm, 18tm, 20tm, 22tm; diluck (planet cartoons); Dima Zel 2bg; Dotted Yeti 14bl, 17tl, 20m, 21t; edobric 23b; Johan Swanepoe 16bg; Jurik Peter 8l, 12bg; Mopic 10b; NASA images 22m; peresanz 9tr; Siberian Art 7r; Triff 11t, 13b; Tristan3D 20bg; Vadim Sadovski 1bg, 4bg, 6bg, 14bg, 18bg, 22bg, 24bg; Vibrant Image Studio 10bg; VikiVector 8tm, 14tm; WP Specialist 10tm; Yindee (astronaut cartoons).

Every effort has been made to trace the copyright holders and we apologise in advance for any unintentional omissions. We would be pleased to insert the appropriate acknowledgement in any subsequent edition of this publication

First published in Great Britain in 2022 by Hungry Tomato Ltd
F1, Old Bakery Studios, Blewetts Wharf, Malpas Road, Truro, Cornwall, TR1 1QH, UK

A CIP catalogue record for this book is available from the British Library

Published and Distributed in India by Scholastic India Pvt. Ltd.

ISBN 978-93-5471-858-8

This reprint edition : January 2025

Printed in India at Shree.Maitrey Printech Pvt. Ltd., Noida